# Atomizer

#  Atomizer

poems

ELIZABETH A. I. POWELL

LOUISIANA STATE UNIVERSITY PRESS • BATON ROUGE

Published by Louisiana State University Press
www.lsupress.org

DESIGNER: Michelle A. Neustrom
TYPEFACES: Whitman, text; Futura, display

Cover image: *Lying Perfume Bottle,* by Laurie Simmons, 1990. Cibachrome print, 48 x 84 inches.
Edition of 5, 2 AP © Laurie Simmons. Courtesy of the artist and Salon 94, New York, NY.

LIBRARY OF CONGRESS CATALOGING-IN-PUBLICATION DATA

Name: Powell, Elizabeth (Poet), author.
Title: Atomizer : poems / Elizabeth A. I. Powell.
Description: Baton Rouge : Louisiana State University Press, [2020] | Includes bibliographical
    references.
Identifiers: LCCN 2020012262 (print) | LCCN 2020012263 (ebook) | ISBN 978-0-8071-7390-9
    (paperback) | ISBN 978-0-8071-7437-1 (pdf) | ISBN 978-0-8071-7438-8 (epub)
Subjects: LCGFT: Poetry.
Classification: LCC PS3616.O8792 A95 2020  (print) | LCC PS3616.O8792  (ebook) |
    DDC 811/.6—dc23
LC record available at https://lccn.loc.gov/2020012262
LC ebook record available at https://lccn.loc.gov/2020012263

This book is not for him or him or him only Him.

I, a universe of atoms, an atom in the universe.

—RICHARD P. FEYNMAN

What I do by involuntary instinct cannot be described.
What I am doing in writing to you? Trying to photograph perfume.

—CLARICE LISPECTOR (TRANSLATED BY IDRA NOVEY)

# CONTENTS

II. HEART NOTES: Patchouli, Bedsheet, Cut Grass, Oak Moss, Burning Hair

III. BASE NOTES: Musk, Steamer Trunk, Ylang-Ylang, Vetiver, Snow

Atomizer

# Atomizer

## 1. TOP NOTES:

Is it right to write about love during the new regime?

I hold my atomizer like a lightsaber. I am learning the kung fu of demure.
I have mastered the koan of coy.

Once upon a time, Yahweh required the incense of burning foreskins, and it
calmed his divinity. First scent, one G-d.

Now scent's top notes introduce an idea, as an initial impression, as a
molecular structure that evaporates quickly, as a memory, as early evening's
enticement, as a cover of a book about online dating and the "end of love."

My atomizer's a DeVilbiss Art Deco made of opalescent glass I inherited from
my flapper great-aunt, it sprays the world out atom by atom.

*(Memory):* Like me she feasted on Lorna Doones and linden tea and strange men.

Fragrance summons angels. I desire Proustian angels, different from
Episcopalian ones.

How to find love? A square space for an uploaded photo, a flirty introduction,
age, height, wants children? *Yes? No?*—Then compulsive gorging on profiles:
"Well travelled. Good kisser. Puts phone away at table. Likes to cook. Techno
not disco. Baseball not football. If you voted for *himself* swipe left."

Love has many scents. He used scent to confound, to throw me off the trail
of who he really was, which may be just another word for emptiness. How
he found the scent that described my memory to my desire and it smelled so
good I had no choice but to love him when his cheek slipped next to mine.

When I smell roses I see hues of blue. Citrus—only yellow. Each petit mal is a
different Rothko painting. Who knew color could smell like rain and the smell
of the rain was apple green?

Then there's the dating site that matches you by your "smell signature": *Wear the same shirt for three days, send it to us, we distribute to possible matches! Voilà!* Holy pheromone.

For all angels are drawn to the one who studies scent as a Rabbi studies the Torah.

Poetry, like argon gas, stabilizes its attar at a faithful temperature.

Come angels. Olfaction is the evocation of memory. Come angels.

Let the atomizer release the top notes of my story, that which evaporates most quickly. Let the atomizer do what it does best: release the distance between autobiography and critical analysis.

I have lost time, and I want it back.

Come angels.


2. HEART NOTES:

And whosoever shall bring me back to the child inside the child, my Matryoshka girl daemon inside me, lure her with whiffs of potions, will lead me anywhere. Trance state.

I am one with the atomizer. We behave differently with different odors: note the limbic system is where memory is utilized, the past inside the whiff and scent of the present.

O, olfactory neurons. Sensory pathway through space and time. Heart notes hold the scent just before the top notes evaporate. Heart notes are the distinctive aspects of perfume, most alluring and charming, most intelligent and clever.

Love has many scents. He used scent to confound, to throw me off the trail of who he really was, which may be just another word for emptiness. How he found the scent that described my memory to my desire and it smelled so good I had no choice but to love him when his cheek slipped next to mine.

*(Memory):* Back on the farm, grandmother supposed the smell of skunk wondrous. I loved the leather smell of cowhide, the salt lick, the watery smells, the lavender and hay rot. This is when she gave me her sister's atomizer.

The cows were in heat some days. I was prepubescent.

*(Memory):* Back home near the city, the bouquet of concrete and locust trees, away from the farm, my mother vanished like top notes of an extinct civet-laced perfume. I roamed our village, locating myself in the perfume shop, gazing in the store mirror for an answer.

*"How may I help you?"*

*(Memory):* The smell of clove, cocoa, and cardamom, the most recognizable. Warm, comforting. Enter Astrid, the shopkeeper, who looked like Ingrid Bergman.

Her perfume store of glass and mirrors and quietude was a kind of church and she was the priestess. I could smell the potions of vetiver and candle wax and iris root.

My apprenticeship: She let me pour the strong galbanums on my wrist to neutralize my fleetingness. I organized the perfume bottles.

I ate squares of cookies, sugar on my fingertips. I felt at home, safe inside the scent of glass. My bubble, my see-through case.

I carried an invisible crown on my head. And whosoever shall bring me back here to this memory will lead me anywhere.

*(Memory):* "You smell the same, that's how I know it's really you."

Imprinted by musks, sniffs of resins, I thought the perfume was a prescription they filled for ailments like loneliness.

Now, the world's best and extinct perfumes are warehoused in the Osmothèque in France, a library for fragrances. It is a kind of Eden.

We lock Eden away because we know we will destroy it. Come angels.

I search for Adam online. To become consumers of smells we must make associations. But we don't have to know a pinecone intimately if we are always smelling Glad pinecone spray for bathrooms.

Indeed, our desire to smell pleasant things is from our lost garden.

The heart of the scent: I have loved men who have hated women.

*(Memory):* their misogyny smelled of lily of the valley.

Come angels.


3. BASE NOTES:

The dark heavy molecules of our base privations late at night.

But sometimes they are also—*we are having a simple chat in the blue stench of ocean breeze.*

Base notes are the subtext.

Base notes are the heavy molecules of scent that stay the longest. They are rich and deep.

Scent is how mates choose. Our immunities lie in our smells. We disperse, for that is our purpose.

*(Memory):* The smell of clinic—heart notes of antiseptic and latex, street clothes and fear, blood musky, rancid and sweet, the stench of scraped cave, of uterus. I have loved men who have wanted me to abort their children.

Fresh lime juice and tequila, a hot D.C. July day. Republicans I have loved, how they canvassed for losers they'd known in frats.

The main body: The smell of oranges and cloves cooked with ham for Christmas. Other seasons, the scent of bay rum, and the pheromones licked from skin: I have loved men who have loved me. Cold water running over warm hands. *Splash.*

In that garden I found I was unclothed. I found I was made from a bone. I was forlorn with snakes. In short, I was afraid. The romance of smell overcame me, scent meant love, and produced spells.

How to find a taxonomy of smells? See Henning's smell prism (spicy, resinous, burnt, floral, fruity, foul) or Linnaeus's seven categories (aromatic, fragrant, ambrosiac, alliaceous, hircine, foul, nauseous).

A formula means to build a form that contains sensual interplays that exist within sense.

*(Memory):* Sometimes we argued under the hot sun of coriander and citrus, or an orchard of pomegranates that tried to set us free from algorithms that market us.

The base notes bring depth, solidity to a scent, an associative connection.

History: modernity is obsessed with commodifying smell.

Sociology: culture is obsessed with commodifying mating.

Love has many scents. He used scent to confound, to throw me off the trail of who he really was, which may be just another word for emptiness. How he found the scent that described my memory to my desire and it smelled so good I had no choice but to love him when his cheek slipped next to mine.

Whatever dissipates, this is what will be left. All top notes now evaporated.

But before there was taxonomy, there was good and there was evil.

This is what I found.

Come angels.

# I. TOP NOTES

Bergamot, Blood, Clouds, Clove, Metal Desk

# The Girl from Ipanema

Walked up to me all the way
from Brazil to serenade my childhood,
all day it was *João Gilberto* and bossa nova,
the samba sang only to me.
Yet, a voice like my mother's began to sing:
*How can he tell her he loves her?*
The music petitioning the afternoon
for mercy. And then, the promise:
*She looks straight ahead not at him.*
My toes in the cold New York Atlantic,
blender-making music on Fire Island,
my father's long coffee-colored fingers,
smelling of limes. The grown-ups fading
into the afternoon's vanishing line. I dragged
the red wagon down the sandy lane, where I walked,
mixture of *flower and mermaid* bossa.
Gilberto and Getz's sonic
thump toward the year of my undoing,
inside the high notes of my long hair
tangling off-key in beach wind and radio sounds.
The song sang of the one chord
Gilberto had played over and over
locked in his bathroom, that year
when everything was changing. How
to understand the new sound of beauty:
How a young girl disappeared into an idea
of a person no one can have.

# When the Insemination Man Comes to the Farm

I

With his tall gray boots, strange protective white
bodysuit as if he were going to do something radioactive,

I'm young; I don't understand; I hide behind hay bales
with the heifers; and we start to grow up.

Impregnation is like having a train coming at you, hitting you, going
in reverse, coming at you again,
hard.

The insemination man with his ramrod, not quite a penis,
threading it through the cervix. All his disgusting canisters.
Never trust a dude in a white van:

Mysterycow juice God in his altar boy paper whites,
the insemination man stalks
my dreams. Wake up girls! I want to scream,
but Grandmother gives me the look.
I will read *The Handmaid's Tale* soon enough.
Twenty years later, I'll invent an eating disorder

where you pump breast milk even after
your baby's weaned, so you can eat
the 500 extra calories. No need for an insemination man.
I am always pregnant and lactating
in my imagination.

II

Small sassy child in coveralls and red bandana, I let
the cows sub in for God, minister to me,
for they have four mighty stomachs

and chew Holy cud. I ask them if
I will marry, and they moo.

And I crawl beside the oldest cow, who
lets me lie next to her, my head on her big belly.
Her long tongue licks the hay of my hair.

I've spent a lifetime not saying what I mean
in order to say what I mean: the art of womanhood in my time,
but I've tried to make it sound serious and smart,
and so I've become a conspiracy theory to my self.
And so I've written letters to the governing body of Starbucks
because everyone knows they make baby formula for grown-ups.

We like our yummy milk, and when
we have lactose intolerance or morals
we make it out of nuts or oats or beans.
We like milk that much.

Poor cow.


III

We delivered a breech calf.
Grandmother's engagement ring slid off
her thin finger inside the mother cow,

so she pushed her hand back in, felt around
until she retrieved it. The vet arriving,
three of us pulling. I fell in the muck. And

one day I will with this ring wed,
when brides will fill the countryside,
and I will tell this story because this barn
is where my life begins;

because this barn was moving
because years were shifting
beneath it. The windows were blurred
with the crying of rain, and the blankets
in the milking room piled like leaves in autumn.

Angelic cows watch over me still, the neglected
child who has forgiven and been
forgiven. All summer has every other summer in it,
like all our hay has alfalfa in it. Everything
seems new at some time. Like the way kisses can.

The ring is gold and is no longer on my finger.
This is my secret marriage: there is no going back to the cow stalls,
or my youth. So, I drink my milk warm and sleep,
and my life begins, wedded again.

# Ars Poetica

My first *real* speech rose scented
        off of a cake of soap,
molecule congealing in my salivary gland
    that held the mellifluous
obscenities I spoke, the words my mother found
horrid, disrespectful, utterances I loved
         and let loose, becoming bubbles
    floating out my mouth
in punishment, the lather bubbling up
    my nasty sentiments:
        how I loved the world so hard I hated it.
Things either clean or dirty,
    smelled lovely or nasty,
my mother tried to make me say it *nicely*. I couldn't.
    The lavender tallow, glycerin atoms ascended
from my lips into silencing
    my words to God,
        which then smelled of Yardley's,
    *Lavandula angustifolia,* disappearing until now.
I try to make it pretty. She never said
    cleanliness was next to Godliness,
    she didn't believe that. She just liked the scent
of lavender and submission,
    hated the words *fuck* and *suck* and *no*.
The molecule of soap a measure that held the grease in my mouth
    called bad words. To make what I felt evaporate
into the bourgeoisie submission of my stink
    into the parfum and titanium oxide
        sanitary normalcy
of control.

# Killing Rabbits

They used to inject women's urine into rabbits to see if the rabbit's ovaries changed. *Yes,* meant pregnant. Either way *the rabbit died,* but the term came to mean: *you are pregnant.*

In Language Arts we learned this: A great rabbit created the world, and a pantheon of 400 rabbits regulates Earth's fertility. They eat many types of sacred lettuces, they sip their milky juices.

I have connectivity between the hemispheres of my brain. I am gaining white matter. My luteinizing hormone is coming out of my pituitary gland like a waterfall. I am estrogen wise. I am hCG (human chorionic gonadotropin) girl: I have killed a rabbit.

Hormones have been changing my body. Hormones make gymnastics more difficult. Tumblesalting with hips, a tipped uterus. Oxytocin releases. I feel love in a world I despise.

Whereas, birth-control pills made me feel like crying at Clash concerts. We use the pullout method instead, though I have read the *Our Bodies, Ourselves* my mother left around for me to find. Her body needs no birth control. Mother doesn't like dicks, she digs estrogen.

I like penises. My father tells me I am like my mother. This is confusing. I shave my armpits. I fuck around, read *Watership Down.*

Oral Contraceptives deplete Vitamin B6, cause disruption in tryptophan metabolism. Growing white-matter creeks in my brain, hCG makes my boobs hurt.

At this moment I am alive twice at once in the rabbit moonlight.

Whereas, on the pill B6 deficiency causes disorders of depression and anxiety and even psychosis. I'm tired all the time. I try to dance. I fool around, read *Watership Down.*

Thinness is necessary for dancing and fucking: I eat lettuces and lettuces, only from my fridge. I read by the rabbit moonlight.

I go to modern dance school. My grandmother is the teacher. Everyone has hairy armpits. I feel my uterus tipping. I have killed a rabbit. Now it is one rabbit. In a few years it will be two rabbits. This is before the abortion clinic bombings and pregnancy tests you can buy at the drug store.

Why must a rabbit die? I look to the moon where the moon rabbit lives, the grim reaper of rabbits who appoints when they will live and die.

Once Peter Rabbit was almost killed in Mr. McGregor's garden. Peter Rabbit ate soporific lettuces. Very sleepy. Large nurses give you something that makes you very sleepy at the clinic, but it is not soporific lettuces.

Disaster: I am sleepy, bloated, and I will never tell my grandmother why I am quitting modern dance. I think I smell: I spray Opium all over my body. How to wear a pad in my Capezio before the invention of "wings." Can't wear my gymsuit there.

Once lettuce was an aphrodisiac, associated with the Egyptian God of Fertility, Min, for resemblance to his very vertical phallus.

Everything I touch wilts, except penises.

Strokes, heart attacks, dizziness, breast tenderness, moodiness.

We use pullout methods.

I am a free woman because I place my legs in stirrups and kill a baby and a rabbit. Full moon that night. We fuck like rabbits, take acid, watch Bugs Bunny, Looney Tunes.

Death is everywhere and pretends to be life, eats too much dirty lettuce.

When I stop bleeding I do flips in the air, hit my hips against the wood of uneven bars in the school gym. Bruise myself for flight. I am a gymnosophist. I flip. The pamphlet in the tiny box of pills says: hormone, anemia, mood swing, dry skin, racing heart, racing thoughts, sweat. Penises: What are they?

Sometimes they wilt like lettuces, mostly they don't.

I don't use birth control because (                              ) I am lonely
and won't understand this for forty years. I don't use birth control, so nothing bad will happen to me in the afterlife, or this life, or in a parallel life. I don't want more hormones. I am not a bioassay test.

Since pregnancy tests have become simplified, no ever says "the rabbit died" anymore.

My Peter Rabbit figurine collection from England and my grandfather's Beatrix Potter books line my bookcase under my Joe Strummer poster.

*Once upon a time there were four little rabbits . . . and a beautiful garden.*

There is a garden one must not go into. It is written.

Side effects: migraines, vision problems. I am not seeing reality correctly. I am the moon's prisoner. Flashbacks or psychosis?

Babies are angels that make heaven open up to me, and I scream on the table lying that I am eighteen though I just turned fifteen. The terror follows me everywhere. A space inside me.

*Once upon a time there were four little rabbits . . . I am sorry to say that Peter was not very well during the evening. His mother put him to bed, and made some chamomile tea; and she gave a dose of it to Peter! One tablespoonful to be taken at bedtime.*

Death, rebirth, D and C. (Blood clots.)
Run. D and C. I die to myself. My bed is bloody.
Rabbits die everyday for lack of what is found.
I crash my car, it flips three times. (Breast tenderness. Dizziness.)

I can't die. And I can't find my parents anywhere. (                    .)
I have killed the rabbit. And it is
          inside me.

# Escape

I

We lived in a small rent-controlled closet.
I was the daughter of lesbians.

There were bats in the attic studying our ellipses.
One flew down like a miniature Lucifer

Stuck in a dark dress made of silky patagium.
I was closeted with them and their silence.

They said: stay inside.
They said: we are not lesbians.

The air smelled of cedar, ashtrays, freezer burn,
Long hot summer. I used to play hide and seek,

But it was an easy place to be found,
And you could get locked in. It was not

Like some wardrobes where you can find
Something out by going in.

Other times it was like a womb. Be quiet,
They said, father might never send a check again,

Mother might lose her job. Sometimes it felt quiet
As a long pause when a story ends about a mother never known

Just before bedtime. A strangely comforting
Silence filled with missed points, three wishes, soup kettles.

I kept the night inside, twisted it like a Rubik's Cube,
So I could better understand the light.

Like after the drunk neighbor got hold of me
When the sun was too high in the sky and I was

Never the same. Sometimes I traced my pencil
In my *Fabulous Book of Mazes* over and over

Looking for exits from dead-end corridors.
Mother was proficient at California walk-ins,

White hatboxes, plastic shoeboxes, clothing
Bags that hung with fancy hotel names and crests.

The creases of slacks sharp, the perfumed scent of sporty blazers,
I searched drawers lined with lavender, found instamatic photos

Of oceans I was not invited to. I don't know why. My mother,
Her girlfriend, and her kids secretly went to the Sound

While I was left home watching my sister and brother
For interminable days without a phone number

Or forwarding address. We pretended
It was an '80's escape room game.

What happens when your Daddy poem
Is about your mother?

I lived as a Madame Alexander doll
Taken out to act correctly.


II


Before this, other '70's mothers exposed their frilly white
Panties, as was the fashion, from under their tennis skirts.

My mother beat them 40–Love.
She was barred. She looked like Billie Jean

King of the tennis court. Shunned, I thought
Because I was bad, mean to my sister, not polite

To my elders, or how I had tried to read
*The Exorcist*. We went visiting on days

off to midcentury modern, tree-lined streets.
I was eight at my classmate's house:

While there our mothers disappeared
And my friend showed me her father's *Joy*

*Of Sex* and went outside. I clamored
Around the house's hallways, opened a door:

My mother and her mother in bed. No one
Said a word, I shut the door.

She pretended I didn't see. She pretended
subtext-plus-shut-up was truth.

There were no angels in our house only demons,
and ripped wallpaper stained with cat pee.

Whatever I saw, she said I didn't see.
Later, my lovers would gaslight me,

That was the legacy. I believed
the opposite. How my mothers used

Perfumery to tell tales about faraway
places with exotic lives.

How can I make this be a feminist text?
The oppressed Lesbian mother should be the hero.

I looked at women from time to time, but it was no use.
I felt nothing. I felt like a disappointment.

We were living in a reticence made of angel/monster
Dichotomy. I became the mad one.

I had anxiety of authorship so long. One summer
I was let out of the secret, sent upstate to her mother's farm.

I had my own stanchion there with the old cow,
Alice, on the urine-soaked hay that gave me a love

For ruinous colognes. For a pillow, Alice's mighty belly
Where I'd listen to the wisdom of her sacred gurgles

During the milking hour at twilight, the time
Mother's girlfriend called *L'Heure Bleue.*

I could leave the stanchion anytime I wanted,
Into the world inseminated with the scent of grass

And grain, warm milk, Betadine solution on udders,
The sweet sting of alfalfa, the sensual world

Of linden trees. I was here, out on good behavior
To this place my mother hated. Heifers jailed in a pen.

Later, she got another place in the city with her secret wife,
Left us sixty miles away in the old closet. I was in charge,

Used laundry quarters for candy bars for dinner.
She'd come back on Tuesday/Thursdays nights,

Take us for pizzaburgers. The silence was the gag rule,
For which there was no Heimlich.

She was just mother's friend.
In an escape room you have to figure out

What in the room is a clue. In college, we talked
For days about *Jane Eyre* and attics. We played "Clue"

In a lounge with windows. I know how the need
To solve for X starts to influence how you perceive

Reality and the resulting adrenaline can be fabulous.
Why look for places to escape from? The room is not

A puzzle, it is a container for the puzzle. Back at the closet,
I was a glass bottle of distilled silence

In an ornate box made of *The Lavender Scare.* My mother
And her girlfriend never abandoned their city apartment

Until they were carried out on long white stretchers
Where their bodies continued to hold that silence

Like a library. And after a long time, I saw free children
In the park playing with their two mothers, marching in freedom

Parades, and I cried. And the vacuumed silence in my head popped.
And one day a window in my heart opened, and I crawled out.

# E-Diptych

My love lives in a tiny, magical box
made of pixels and engineering. When I write him
he writes me back, and when he writes me
back, I write him. Though we exist
me, him, here, there: one day our band
of consciousness will transmigrate,
when science puts chips in brains,
every mystery intimate as sweat.
For now, imagination's a gangling vine
clings to life. He's been so busy
writing a narrative where he has no wife,
she vanished in no time. So much first-person
construct and banter: he has
a vixen schoolteacher held down
on his mind's featherbed. And when he
writes me, he makes me,
and when I make him, I write him.
We are invented, by the wanting
and not having of others. Soon, someone else
will pick him from his little box
and begin again, waiting for him
in the rain outside the coffee shop,
where donuts harden the way he can't,
and the red vinyl stool swirls empty
as if trying to conjure something so close.
But so close is almost, and almost
is still a climax too far—for
*if* is further than you think.
She tries to pick him out of the crowd,
ever hopeful, though night comes on like an emergency.
We live two places at once, virtual and real. My love
lives in a little box. Someone
is making him
into something else now.

## II. CHEMISTRY.COM—HE'S A MATCH

I know you really wanted to meet me,
but I had the sneaky feeling you were an über
Aryan chiropractor with autoerotic
tendencies, that maybe I should re-up
with my academic Asperger's husband,
wear muumuus on Saturday nights.
You live in this little box spread across
the screen of pixelated desires.
But I met you, before your snowboard race
the style gel in your crew cut looked like ice,
and you, disappointed my hair
didn't match my photograph,
implied I lied as we walked Stowe's
Main Street, past flatlander tourists buying
scented candles, and Gnostic punk rock
townies eating baguettes,
my nose running in the cold,
until we came to the cemetery and after you
maligned your lying ex-wife,
lamented your pretty old girlfriend,
and waxed overly cute about a pair
of little green baby shoes that made you realize
you were now too old for children. I parsed the poetic
significance of shoes, how used and alone,
they symbolized death. Your text messages
beeped us all the way to my car, German,
but not clean, where you wished me good luck,
shook my ungloved hand, then thought better—
and hugged me as if you were Princess Diana,
and I, a grateful patient in the ward.

# In the Shadow

Of Mount Mansfield we all have *Bernie* stickers on our bumpers,
and dents in our hearts, brains, bank accounts, what we have left
of our jobs. *The Nightly News:* a conspiracy of rapid gunfire,
police brutality, ISIS, North Korea. Where is the story about the bird
I saw yesterday filing a complaint against the school board
for the cutting of music, recess, running in the green wonder out back?
Once we went to see a ballet recital, everyone was a sunflower
that day. The F-16s overhead stunned the great green Vermont
mountain above us. We are always at war now.
We don't know when to be alarmed.
The sound strikes out the crack of the home run
some kid hit over the fence. You say: *can you please repeat*
*what you just said?* I couldn't hear you.
It doesn't matter. We say the same thing
over and over and wonder what country we are in now.
I grade essays about stream-of-consciousness.
Once we climbed the 4,000 feet of this on a sun-foliaged day
like people who believed in maple trees, wild blueberries.
The television is a liquor cabinet to which we will retreat
after dinner. Change the channel, change your liquor:
beer before liquor never sicker. Everything's a craft
cocktail or locally sourced. Even you are
a diversity of identities and it has made you weird
as if you have smoked so much individuality pot.
We drink-watch the night claim our mountain,
and the baseball game falls asleep. I used to love
everyone. There's been a lot of neo-cosmic activity
going on; now we qualify for the privilege
of food stamps and heating assistance.
There have been four UFO sightings
since last week, and the newscaster
is married to the pretty lady in my church
who knits with her own lamb's wool,
so what he says must be true.

# The Box

If you can't all agree on what to watch, I'm going to throw
this damned thing out the window.

—MOTHER, 1978

The TV says it loves me best in an emergency or a natural disaster. The TV
asks how many are injured. The TV tells me I will vote for Hillary because I'm
X age, with Y beliefs, *and* I don't use the C word. The TV says it doesn't like it
when my mother calls it the Idiot Box. The TV warns me of erections lasting
more than four hours, and wants us all to have bathtubs with mountain views.
The TV sings the national anthem and uncovers crying babies needing Gerber
baby food, nothing else will help. The TV tells me not to read *The New York
Times*. And for a moment I have to agree with the TV. The TV has some new
jingles with a backbeat, and a secret message that will make me do wonderful
things-if only I would just listen. The TV confirms my worst fears: I have
spent too much on my life insurance policies. The TV implies George Clooney
is the smartest man left on earth, but I know this to be untrue. The TV agrees
with George Clooney that only women half his age can suck his big fat dick.
The TV says a man came out of nowhere wearing a hoodie. The TV asks me
why I believe in white privilege. The TV implores me to shave my genitals.
The TV prefers breast meat, and has found a way for everything to be breast
meat. The TV asks me to consider having people from other cultures over to
eat frozen pizza and drink wine from long-stemmed glasses that I can buy not
far from here, that it will make me more interesting. The TV says don't leave
me, I can be anyone. The TV says I remember you as a child, how sad and
lonely you were, how bereft. The TV says I should stop trying to make sense
of what it is saying, that to do so will increase my blood pressure, cause tingly
feet and perhaps fainting. The TV is downloading a better self inside my self,
and for this I try to be grateful. The TV tries to understand irony. The TV says
it is the mother I never had. The TV calms my stomach. The TV is having a
tumultuous affair with Donald Trump and blames me for watching. The TV
knows exactly how much I don't know. The TV believes in loud public music,
and not just in elevators anymore. The TV will deliver me flowers for the meal
it shows me how to throw together. The TV will make my hair curly. The TV
has dogs who really speak and babies, too. The TV tells me not to tell anybody
what the TV says. The TV has turned the family into an audience. The TV
says sportsmanship at values.com. The TV says large plastic bags with lots of

plastic shit. The TV says a tiger killed a zookeeper. The TV says blonde hair, big boobs. The TV is obsessed with breasts not just breast meat. The TV tells me it remembers when I was crazy in the rocking chair with postpartum, how it kept me company by keeping me scared. The TV said, your life in minutes, hours, seconds. The TV put a Band-Aid on my eyeball. The TV sings its angelic white noise. The TV uses a *strategy of indirection*. The TV says Russian prostitutes said so, and the revolution will not be televised. The TV makes like it is friends with Jane Goodall, Big Papi, Obama, God. I have known the TV for forty-five years now, and it has watched me cry, pee, cook, fuck, clean: sometimes I'm not sure who the voyeur is anymore. The TV who remembers my dead mother to me, how she threatened to throw it out the window a long time ago now, but that TV is dead too, long having Coke poured into its vents by my irate brother watching Howard Cosell narrate the *Wide World of Sports,* and a knob that fell off into nowhere. When one of us was stoned. The TV says that old TV is probably space-junk now in outer space, catching cable signals for free, avoiding the Russians. The TV says that little TV is never coming back, so I should quit my crying.

# At Old Yankee Stadium

The Bronx burned and the Mayor, Ed Koch, got his picture taken
With my imaginary husband because he was the bat boy
For the Yankees. We watched baseball most of 1977.
Catfish Hunter threw a ball at everything I didn't like
And tried to smash it. I said: the problem with time is time.
I said this because the imaginary isn't always linear.
Baseball is never the problem, mostly the solution.
There is no buzzer in baseball.
Everyone you love is everyone you love in 1977
Because we hadn't invented ironic distance yet.
My imaginary husband was on the plane with Thurman Munson,
Like baseball he was beyond death. 7-7-77
We got hitched in the dugout, Billy Martin officiating,
Taking the cross from his cap, making us both
Kiss it. My imaginary husband was Catholic,
I wasn't. The heat kept climbing and I was scared;
The minutes congealed into the footage
Of the game before it looked old.
We had our imaginary baby the next miracle
October, named him Reggie for the homeruns.
But first the lights went out and the trouble
Started with the real, and my imaginary husband stayed
Out late ransacking the streets. While things burned
The rain stopped working, so that
No one knew what was what anymore.
My mother became a man and didn't understand
My imaginary husband. *No such thing*
*As gender,* she said. *No such thing as real,* quoth I.
*Melissa Ludtke's in the locker room,* (s)he said.
*And girls can join little league now, you know.*
My mood ring was purple most of the time, which meant
I was becoming more visible with a kind of looting intensity,
Like the great silence of my imaginary husband
Rounding the bases, sliding so fast into home
He made the present emerge right here,
The old stadium gone.

# The Ordinary Odor of Reality

Is as strong as our bones
steeped in our bodies
like Red Rose Tea.
Outer space smells like rum,
so says spectral analysis,
but all my trauma reeks of
baby powder and chlorine.
We breathe 86,400 times a day.
We ingest each other through
our nostrils straight into
our amygdala like '80's cocaine or salt
water over our heads. I have inhaled
my worldview from the sterility
of Brutalist architecture, schoolrooms
I have sat in. I am having a smell dialogue
with mold and wet earth and sand
that resides in the woods and playground
inside my memory. What are
your odor threat cues? Coolant? Match
strike? Summer day? All arranged
in form, a story? I put on
the Olfactory Virtual Reality
Headset that looks like space goggles
with a scent-o-graph that changes
with each virtual image, in order
to confront the Aqua Velva, polyester
bedspread, peppermint schnapps,
urine and semen and tobacco,
the capture and pillage
of my seventh year. Now
in warrior headdress, I combat
the reality of the moment
that launched my career
in PTSD. Cyberpsychological
treatment, imaginal exposure
therapy to locate the past

so, I can crash back through,
on a treadmill with my space goggles
and therapist, and relive it
to master it, and take a shovel
to rebury it in that wet earth,
but without me.

# In Vilnius

—for my Daughter

I

I drink tea with cream in the Old City away
from my new love, who is now my old love.
I type and pull the hair
away from my face
as my Grandmother might
have. It is morning turning into
afternoon in the Old City.
I am drinking tea with cream.
I am wearing glasses and lipstick and my age.
I am wearing the past made of baizing
and the future made of spring.
I am riding a horse into my sleep and back.
I found out who I am by being who I am.
I am Shulammite and Dynamite,
and the hours haven't worn me away.
I don't like the past
how it crashes down on the land,
a meteor, yet the hours have made me,
a refugee's descendant. I am looking at
my great grandparents' apartment
house. I am on vacation.
It was frequently noon.
It was frequently time for lunch.
It was frequently Jerusalem,
but not territory. It was
a momentous occasion,
but it was very plain,
plainer than linen, stronger
than aquavit, than a tree-lined street.
I kept trying not to fall asleep.
I kept telling myself not to age.
I kept at it, and was it, and wasn't it.

II

What was *it* I'm to do to deserve this
peace. *It* took me a long time.
*It* took me in its arms.
*It* said I was It, and It knew me
before I knew it.
Its reflection surfaced in windows
all around me.
It was enveloped by fog,
and the river and Olandu Street.
It was the Old City and the river beneath it.
It came to me in the night saying *it it it itititititit,*
and I tried to know it
until I knew *it.*
*It* was revelatory, hiding in
all the things I saw:
The Yiddish theater,
the Forest at Paneriai.
I will be here until I am not here.
I was so tired I woke up into another
life that was the same life,
but better.
It was delightful.
It was Sholem Aleichem.
It was magnificent like light blossoming
rose-flecked in June.
It smelled of barbed wired turning to sprigs of wild mint.
The temple smelled of myrrh and balsam and silence.
When I spoke to my life in the Old City
the song sang: *It said it is,*
*it was, it will be.* When I talked to my life,
when I talked to my life, I became my life
and the more I became my life

the more I talked to my life,
and my life sang the old Partisan Song
so that I might really live:
*Therefore never say the road now ends*
*for you, though leaden skies may cover over days*
*blue. Our step beats out the message:*

*We are here.*


III


And so I saw. And the afternoon
lolled on until it too became
a glorious pain or a vanity or a bike ride,
pedaling away minutes. I made sure
I had a map of the Old City.
I had the log of all the names related
to my name: Isaac Shalit, Rose Brazil
I had my name. I had the street
number and street my great grandparents lived
on, though the numbers might have been
different, changed, but
I was resourceful, I was curious,
I was alive,
and I knew *it* and *it* was known.

# Shulammite

One day I stopped the swipe,
        left or right. One day
I started to believe
        like the Shulammite,
the ashen-haired ancestor
        that *I am my Beloved's*
*and his desire is toward me,*

whether I ask for it or not
        because that's what faith is
because that's what Shulammite means:
        *O, Daughters of Zion.*
The time for singing has come. His name's
        perfume, and it pours out on my name.

This truth procedure
        is a composition that is not
of the forefinger and a screen and a selfie stick.
        A society of love cannot be proven
in three sporty photos, a yoga pose,
        a bike ride in Vermont, a car selfie.

The more I swiped, the more love eluded
        me. Come away from your computing
children. Truth is the oar in the water.
        The hand gripping. Belief
is the birdcall of Saints.
        For the screen does not blossom
forth frankincense or liquid myrrh.

Many are sad because of their screens.
        So, I will sing to my Beloved
of how I was delivered from the dynamite
        of the Tinder, the flame of false

desires, marketed kisses, the sighting,
        the sending off. A match
that cannot ignite. My life

to blast to the core of coquetries' online
        presences. How I still wear scent
as homecoming. Aldehyde: Chanel No. 5.
        His song forms time and his breath
smells of apples and calamus. I adjured him:
        *turn your eyes away from me,*
they overwhelm me! Do not stir up love
        until it is ready!

So, my beloved gathers
        his myrrh with my spice,
his Patou pour Homme, with my Chanel Cristalle,
        his Dior Fahrenheit; with my Bal à Versailles girlhood
civet-laced and dark in a Parisian bottle.
        O, Daughters of Zion,
the gazelles and does rise to the summit
        during the harvest moon,

unsubscribe to dating sites scribed
        by people who don't believe. For even
the moldering hay knows it is sung
        in the wind *not to awaken love*
*until it is ready.*

For did not my people die of the wages of love?
        Yes, my people died of the wages of love.
Yet, here I am. Did they not traverse the desert, too?
        Yes, and did they not thirst?
Yes, they did not thirst.

*For Beloved, for you are the scent*
          *between my breasts.* I will no longer trust
the vagary of electronic nothing, for I am
          of the Shulammite's line, her attar of mandrake
rises in me like testimony, like law. I lay it
          at the other altar of: He comes,
without doubt, without swipe right, without type,

without facial recognition, without thumbprint:
          *For I am my beloved's and his desire*
*is for me and it gives forth fragrance*
          *his myrrh and my spice.* Who writes?
Who conjures? My Beloved contains all
          of Solomon's Songs, his ylang-ylang fills
the hidden scroll inside me,

and I write the first part of the sentence,
          and he completes it, and all his scents seize me,
and I believe there is nothing
          more to believe but, O Daughters of Zion,
his eyes do not turn away.

# Burlington Is Nuts Today

for Angi Palm

This is why I moved to the country?
Everyday is a hipster convention. Girl with $300 jeans,
sports her "ANTIFA" t-shirt and cork-heeled shoes.
I agree with her, but, but, but . . .
I would like some $300 jeans. Maybe. I think
of the poem "Sir Patrick Spens": I have grown inpatient, I mean
impatient. Fake farmers in overalls selling their window-grown wheatgrass.
I'm stuck in a huge backup of cars that want into our taxpayer-
funded parking garage for people who only use credit cards—
this used to be Vermont now it is the Upper West Side.
I keep pushing the button for a ticket. Moms
with unsymmetrical haircuts drag their helicoptered children
in Birkenstocks toward home where the world was ending
on CNN just moments ago. A white dude on smack
wretches junk sick into the trashcan. A handsome
professor in Danish glasses and a brief case
looks on disapproving. I fear I am getting fat
and vulnerable. I think mean. In a bad mood. No longer
so pretty. My name itself makes a scratchy sound.
The dude who was my 100-percent match,
and is unobtainable, says he "smashes patriarchy," too.
I myself am skunked. The construction guy crunches
toward the hard core of his lunch, almost over. His rich parents
in Canada funded his grad degree with high hopes. I'm late for coffee
with the young Elizabeth Taylor of nonfiction.
I like to witness her youth and hope she gets everything
she thinks she wants. Later tonight, Rachel Maddow will pull
up the shade only to find more darkness. The world is ending,
boy scouts, hippies: Take a ticket,
have it validated since you can't be—short-term
parking is full. Now, please pull the ticket out: *Proceed.*

# Lying Perfume Bottle of Chanel Pour Monsieur

"Tell me everything," he said.
That was the top note, that was
what the scent would have said
if it could also speak nouns, *window, sun,*
*woman, summer,* filling the white-walled bistro.

How oakmossy the world is,
how odor is identity's first ardor.
His scent opens, a portal. He said I seemed
worthy of its lemony neroli blessings,
its Coco philosophy *of my life*
*didn't please me so I created my life.*

The light wafts in the window, inflects
the room with Vermont in June, languidly
arriving on dust motes: I am an object,
ponging myself into capture's mendacities.
His antediluvian cardamom yanks me,
a jazz song my father listened to or a shape

no geometry understands. There's something familiar
about the animalic scent, the refined contradiction
of all that presses into my plasticine skin. Not all
scents register in the conscious mind. I hope to seize
his chypre accords inside me, like Arcturus flickering.
Reader, even the sky has a composition.

He sips espresso, eats blueberries—
his citrusy spell flirts the morning air, he plays
the *beaux ideal* elegantly. Now you *tell me*
*everything*—I want the aromatics: how the blooming
foliage comes over me like a perfume bottle's
glass enclosure. I see out: a Friday morning,

the polite ambition of lovers. This memory
an atomizer I'm sprayed out of, droplets seep into pores:
*Tell me everything.* He said it was advertised
as a gentleman's scent, in 1955, to open over a whole day.
How it adorned Mad Men and rogue Dukes-of-Thus-
and-Such. Fantasy is what we create when we have nothing

left to say about a world that has left us trendy,
fetishized, and empty. He researched me as an olfactory
curator might, my social media Lysol life,
how to turn moments into hyperrealism.
Daughter of the cold hard sell. *Tell me everything.*

My father wearing this scent, tightening his tie,
his capitalist's noose, thinking he's 007, slapping
himself in the face, no woman can know him.

# The Book of Sires

I

In reality it was a semen catalogue
a print precursor to online
dating, but for cows. The barn's romance
filled with the stench of nitrogen,
Gram's back to the land ambitions,
her own mating disappointments,
the milking room radio remunerating
Chopin's Preludes to barn cats
amid the promise of herd genetic
progress and economic relevance.

She studied the book with weird affection,
attentive predilection. She'd semaphore
the insemination man which bulls
to mate with her Holsteins, calf-weaned,
unsuspecting on the moors, to make
the best milkers, obtain prestige,

as her own mother from Chicago
society picked a Harvard man.
Instead, Gram swapped husbands
with a friend, quickly divorced,
remarried in Hidalgo.
And the wisdom passed to me
with her engagement ring: don't stay
in bed late on Sundays,
unless you want a big family.
Perhaps in her blue jeans and red kerchief
she was teaching me—her preteen
string bean, the best way
to propagate is at a distance where
you can't smell the raw stench
of sex, where it is practical,
based on actual data
for mating.

II

I found him, online
displayed as if in a "Book
of Sires." I was in heat.
It was August sweaty.
I could not retreat.
The irony wasn't lost on me,
how he managed the air
above waste dumps, making sure
the levels didn't go above
the permitted micrograms
per year. My homage:
He was an atelier of garbage.
How his microaggressions
of Paco Rabanne were really
endocrine disruptors, phthalates
from petrochemicals he studied

in the lab. Perfume is a code:
I will change my allure
chemically. But then
a friend sent me an article;
"The New Secondhand Smoke."
"Per"—through, "Fumus"—smoke.
Perfume was killing us, too.
For to perfume is to cover up truth,

like the way the Oscar Mayer factory
used to scent the air all around
Madison, Wisconsin, with fake sweet,
strawberry scent, so no one thought
about the entrails and bones of those bulls
and their tortured burning.

# Umpire

Everyone is losing their attention span, for baseball and for love.
It's the end of romance. Swiping left or right all night: yet,
on a sidewalk in Johnson, Vermont, I put my leather
jacket in your car. It's sexy how your trunk holds
a pitch indicator, a chest protector, low top turf shoes, a uniform
designed to appease our need to keep the world—*safe,*
order out of disorder. How a 1980's boom box on Jones Beach
once punk-yodeled, Gang of Four: *I love a man in a uniform.*
A fair game, I'm living the questions, watching each base. I delight
in how your dating profile is the only one
that pays attention to who is on first, so straight ahead
about the trouble of commodifying what might be,
saying you like to argue about Marxism, craft beer, this game.
For Christ's Sake, I love how you can make a decision.
*This game:* I hate how players can injure with fake-out tags.
I don't totally cotton onto what you mean when you say your strike
zone is out, you seem right on to me. You're almost
a whole foot taller than I, enveloping like the stadium
shades the field late in the day. You know what an umpire knows:
rules, how to communicate, be decisive, unaffected. I like
how you can see above the whole blessed green,
make a decision, size a moment up, that you're willing
to call it whatever *it* is, error, double play, or not.
I don't even know if I'll like your calls yet, though you love
what I love: Whitman, Joe Strummer, staggeringly
Thurman Munson, who caught my childhood in his glove
like a God. And when he died I cried on the stoop
with the boys. You're the handsome pope of baseball, making
sure theology is sensible, what's okay, what's not.
You're the fresh prince of verges and thresholds,
able to crouch down at the plate and say, "You're out!"
How exciting! How this game is made of the great mystery
that never allows us to be sure we will ever get home, that place
made of score and safety. How I yearn to hear you call

the plays, but there is much I don't know: o, dumb metaphor,
errors or not, I slide, feet first, in this tangible world, hyped, but
made of air and dust, advancing toward what—
winning or losing as we must?

# Hidden in Plain Sight

One day the mentalis muscle in his face changes,

only slightly. Then his tongue tastes different.

Whatever is seen cannot be unseen.

He's begun texting in the john—

keeping his phone in his pajama pocket,

travels unexpectedly: New York, Chicago, Rio de Janeiro.

Early May June July you notice—

*no ideas but in things*—

the shift in his friend's conversations, the blooming desire of trees,

placement of his water glass by the window.

It's not the obscure that makes us lose

our way, it's when the fearless leader plays us

his theme song at rallies, "Sympathy for the Devil,"

and we don't take him at his word.

The Tao of the unanswered questions

remains hidden until there is no going back,

and it happens the way dusk suddenly is darkness,

and our eyes adjust.

# Spritz

Was what my mother called sweating. *We spritz, we don't sweat.*
What about *skank?* So exotic. Rules for nice girls—*Don't wear nylon*
　　　*drawers.* The smell of white cotton panties, fresh
from the line is best. Go for nuance of honey and cumin. Don't be catcalled—
　　　*catfish.* Arousal is a communication the body makes. As a child the smell
of mud and cinnamon soothed my sunburns. Now at night when
　　　tendril musks bloom patchouli, my body does the Lindy.
Whatever signal my respiration plus heartbeat plus endocrine
　　　chemicals publicize, I attract strange bedfellows. Even the bees
pollinating roses and jasmine for endnotes know
　　　the olfactory signatures of their own group. We communicate
through scent, we don't walk blindly toward the plank of love.
　　　Trigger identification, primordial emotion: Big Brother knows
how to market that in synthetic pheromone molecules of a billion dollar industry.
　　　Once, I tried smell dating: wore a T-shirt three days and nights,
then took it off, sent it to Smell Dating central,
　　　where they cut the shirt in pieces, mailed out to prospective suitors
for them to smell, identify which appealed, see if my choice matched theirs,
　　　*voila,* ode to our limbic system *cha cha cha* over a martini or espresso
in a darling bistro where pheromone baits trap gypsy moths.
　　　History shows my ovulation triggered spermatozoa wars.
In the mornings washing with Cashmere Bouquet,
　　　I make *it* new like a car. In my kimono and red lipstick
I read the papers in bed. But at 9:51 a.m. I go back to the idea:
　　　*Perfume is the feeling of flowers,* a prayer burning
like brandy down the gullet. Poor flowers,
　　　how shall they avoid their feelings? I read Glück's *The Wild Iris,*
study their voices. I keep scents I never wear
　　　like "Love's Baby Fresh" circa 1976. It's like keeping a specimen
of a lie in a bottle. Forcing yourself to love a perfume
　　　is like forcing yourself to love someone you don't.

# An Alabaster Jar of Nard

after a painting by Jean Beraud, *St. Mary Magdalene in the House of Simon the Pharisee,* 1891

Jesus loves me, but he also loves other women.

This is hard for me to reconcile. I am not polyamorous.

What, I wonder, would the Pharisees say around this table

at Simon's house, dressed in Victorian evening clothes, tails and bow ties,

their handkerchiefs scented with Houbigant Fougère

looking down on a Parisienne Mary Magdalene prostrate over Jesus's feet,

a Jesus modeled after a socialist, not dressed in proper evening attire?

When you get old enough everything is either parable or social mockery.


Here, this Jesus, is the summer sensation of the Champs de Mar

exhibition. "Do you see this woman?" Jesus is busy telling the men

the parable of the two debtors. On the floor Mary tries

to shun her sexual slavery in a gossamer evening dress,

a Worth or a Doucet. Beauty isn't always redemption.

The men think she is having a temper tantrum, spoiled girl.

Jesus's love is like incense touching every crevice. Mary knows this:

Sometimes you have to smash open a vessel that holds what you thought was
   valuable

to become, to be. When the perfume of nard releases its top notes,

most volatile, they evaporate quickly into this biblical story.


In this Belle Époque dining room, Jesus's feet are clean and smell nice for now.

The men around Jesus at the table with a crisp white Parisian bistro cloth,

back from the opera, having strolled by the Seine, where years before Baudelaire

imagined someone might name a perfume after him one day, seeing deep

into the postmodern where his scent namesake translated *"memories and emotions*

*into products and experiences"* a *"limitless brand universe"* gotten to through

his own Voyage, his *"lazy isle to which nature has given singular trees, savory fruits,*

*men with bodies vigorous and slender, women in whose eyes show a luminous candor."*


But it is no sensational Belle Époque here on Hunger Mountain in raw November.

My batterer boyfriend unbuttons his Oxford, my face lies there,

a Veronica of Lancôme bronzer on his white undershirt.

I trace his sternum with my index finger. I am painting him

like these biblical characters in Beraud's contemporary situations.

Insight can start simply, like: *I would like to arrive, finally, at home.*

*Like in a kitchen with a book, or a TV room.* What is nard, anyway? I say to him.


On the bed, the book still open to this painting, the old Bible story where Mary

uses the very last of her expensive nard in an alabaster jar;

soaks each shaft of hair to wash the savior's feet. It's an extravagant

perfume, biblically old, still in fashion. From, the *Nardostachys*

*jatamansi*, it's an ancient, aromatic amber-colored oil for anointing.

A waste of money, he says. He knows nothing. I think about the parables

of love where the sins are many and forgiven, when one has loved much.

And all I can think is that *Jesus loves me, but he also loves*

*this other woman*, healed as I thought I could never be and, thus,

she must be better than me. I must stop making men my Gods.

# II. HEART NOTES

Patchouli, Bedsheet, Cut Grass, Oak Moss, Burning Hair

# Things that Aren't Good

Your other dream of ripping off my face to make it yours
waits for you at the bus stop. The television ads enumerate
the myriad ways I've been undone
by drug companies, the government, stupid ass bitches,
you. 7/8 of everything incubating beneath the surface.
No one has told the television about you. *Sorry.*
Your therapist alerts you about your parents,
how they might be liable. You look out
the café window: so many just-divorced
yoga yummy-mommies there
for the taking. You salivate over dating
sites like porn, until you fall into
Ativan and Ambien REM drool. *Sorry.*
Your poorly curated hanging plants
might suffocate you in your sleep if you can't stop
buying perfume on e-bay and pretending you know
how to sail. Once you seemed to be
the handsome fantasy I cut
from magazines for teen collages;
I don't think they prescribe Prozac for this.
It won't help. Neither will
reading *Man's Search For Meaning. Sorry.*
What does a hero do if he doesn't break,
plunder, quest? Not even the election results startle you.
Our yearning is a kind of loss, a desire never filled.
Breathing is synching the iPod
that has recorded my heartbeat,
and remembered your thumbprint.
What is it to want things
that are not good for you?
I will practice sudden resurrection. *Sorry.*
Each morning I do it again, which means
I had to die the night before.

# Self-Portrait: Smell Me

after Martynka Wawrzyniak's art installation *Smell Me*

Egg yolk, frozen eyelashes, angel skin with petrichor and geosmin, tang
of metallic blood, Hudson River, long train, empty Whitman's Sampler, rain
on Sunday, yellow taxicab, Cointreau flambé, lemon wax, sawdust, mailbox,
early snow and roasting chestnuts, my reincarnation—fifteenth life, Bear
Mountain, needlepoint basket, hibernal bed sheets in pink, wet parsley, field
hockey sticks, cheerleading sweat, old Turner Classic Movie tears, a memory
ten carbons long, a ghost from three weeks ago, news ink, plums sautéed
in brandy and butter, transatlantic flight with dinner service, hot dish rag,
transient inkling, Clinique lipstick in the bathroom of the Met, Holy Ghost,
Grandmother's old love letters, rain on tin, hay in sun, cucumbers sweating
on buttered bread, burnt sugar and candied violets, cool bathwater with ivory
soap, monogrammed red wool sweater from college, pencil eraser, mason
jar of old bone buttons, leather valise, salt funk all night, new white socks,
moldered hymnal, *Lunch Poems* on the screened in porch, clouds, *a flower with
no scent and stronger than a gun*, adrenaline, a twice-worn nightshirt.

# Cinema Verité

*. . . depends on the art of telling yourself lies.*
—JEAN ROUCH

SCENE 1

Smoothing his hair from his face, he approved his appearance in the
darkened window. A snowflake of frost spidered itself on the glass, but he was
hot from jalapeño martinis, though his wife's Connecticut blue eyes held him
like a leash. The party Babbled like the tower. The Christmas tree shimmered.
His phone vibrated in his pocket. He liked being watched. A young hottie in
blue-green sequins drifted mermaid-like across the party. How he longed to
hear her say, *Come live with me and be my love.* Her Victoria's Secret breasts,
her oceany allure. The blue glass collection on the sill quivered with the high-
pitched ruin vibrating from his solar plexuses. He decided to pat her naiad
ass so softly, so prep-school politely, wife-y would never know. How he loved
being naughty, and how being naughty loved him. He stared into the Yule log,
and it cracked open his vanity. It stoked him when disaster winked at him. The
partygoers could all read his narrative: see the Buckley marriage fall apart. Yet,
he liked his wife after the party smelling of toothpaste and anti-aging serum
curled up in bed next to him, her cold feet between his shins—a hundred
white Christmas lights up his spine—so cold they were blistering him like
liquid nitrogen, ready to catch fire.

SCENE 2

What a piece! He thought of a fortune cookie fortune he might write:
He who attends his boss's wedding shall yield a thousand cherry blossoms
in bounty. An embossed invitation: welcome to eternal spring and all her
goddesses more fruitful than all the blondes in Bendel's at lunch hour. She—
imagination—made permanent. Last night, he had dreamt of her Ledean body
rising like the sudden quadrupling of pure cash. What was happening to him?
He was psychic gaga over this chick. What narration and consolation to be
this unhinged. The certain heaven and life everlasting of the greenback, and
now this—five-foot-two-eyes-of-blue. Her daddy on the Fortune 500, that
postulation of power. And now the night coming down on him like the pearly

gates of her perfect, plump mouth. For this no witchcraft could undo him; he is prepared by all rights, the rights he has been endowed with by Shearson, Lehman, American Express Trust Management. The inner workings of fate have given him this opportunity to jet set himself about her boudoir in randy boxer shorts made of silk—oh, he hopes. Her tresses and distresses hung out a window to dry in his sun. The mercy of cash accounts. The might of his fixed-up flesh. To breed, finally, to breed his name. Yes, he will be her priest and her vanity. Little kitten draw near, he purrs, the claws of his mind, the vodka tonic of his blood.

## SCENE 3

In the beginning: she hit him with a plastic dart. Lacking intoxication, she used accident as an excuse—though she was glad to have hit him. She apologized as if she meant it. She liked that he thought it funny, amusing. She didn't care if the other patrons found her aggravating. She liked this dive, its odor of yeast and sweat, her sense of treading some unnamed risk. None of her friends would be caught dead here. She wanted to buy him a drink, and say, *they're playing our song,* but he merely winked at her, pulling his big, black leather coat over his shoulders, nodding in her direction—a nod that made her evaluate all nods for the next three days, to distinguish if they could merely mean *goodbye,* or if they could mean *hello.*

## SCENE 4

Filing her nails with the perseverance of the annoyed, all she could think of was how tired she was from taking care of everything, every detail in their life together. Even the cars. She didn't subscribe to gender roles, but enough was enough. Why couldn't he deal with the cars? Whenever she brought the station wagon in for an oil change, they always tried to sell her extra things she didn't need, and she knew if she got them her husband would be upset. Her ponytail so tight it looked like her hairline might recede any moment from the force of it.

Knocked up at twenty, after previous abortions, she hadn't wanted to test her luck with a Lord she wasn't totally sure didn't exist. She had left her local progressive radio station to marry the teaching assistant from her mass communications class. He was the one who had knocked her up. Now, twelve years later, she knew there was indeed a God and his main purpose was to torture her. She knew that seemed self-important to think, but her husband was balding, now overweight, still sleeping with his students. He did it the way many women eat chocolate: compulsively, secretly, with great melt-in-the-mouth relish.

She no longer even realized when men looked at her, until she saw him. He must be the new guy, she thought, his sweaty coveralls in the greasy light, a patchouli and oil-rigged smell gurgling from him. She had neglected to find out his name, the way he put his greasy palm print on her face, the way she licked the roof of his mouth, the way it tasted of new car smell and licorice.


SCENE 5

At Gate 33 in Terminal C, he was typing something into his laptop, commanding his universe through the thin sheaf of metal at his ear. She was tired of her fiancé's tenderness. To be with an animal like this guy, someone who wouldn't let a deal lie fallow. Her jet-lag exhaustion unnerved her. Still, she wanted to travel straight into his micromanagement through the thin internet cable of possibility.

Good fortune had thus eluded her. Tick-tock. She felt it would forever elude Thomas at home with his art auctions and eighteenth-century furniture and homemade jams. So unlike this man, his sturdy, Italian leather wingtips enduring all marches. Lately, she understood what it meant for one to want to enlist in an army, to be under command. With her wishing, she pressed her sexual everything against his flat screen to deposit there in the gigabytes, to pop open like an advertisement. Just then, his green eyes surveying the world for just the right kind of legs.

## A Warning

He said what I wanted him to say, but the words came so fast.

The silence after he said it. The silence not looking at me. The not looking.

And I remembered how he used the same phrase we heard on NPR weeks ago—

as if rehearsing a scene. There was a sort of harshness in the way he parked the car.

His fingertips on the wheel. His nails so perfect they masked an imperfection.

*Don't touch that*, he said. I left my visor down.

He had scents for every occasion—fougères, orientals, gourmands.

He had costumes for everything—bright orange jumpsuit for chainsawing,

special non-slip booties for sailing, the black racing spandex of a bicyclist.

On the back of the car the bike wheels rolled counterclockwise and furiously.

The way he was enunciating everything perfectly

made my clothing feel too tight, as if

his speech, like bad perfume, would never come off.

# Portrait of Woman in Bath

There is no cure for phantom odors.
All that summer an olfactory mirage,
specter scents of climbing roses
molting their delirium through
my blowing curtains—the aroma
of burning hair, leather horsewhip, diesel.
My mother said I had phantosmia,
as she wash-clothed my thinking
into whatever she wanted,
smelling whatever she smelled.
I floated until she said
the soap bubbles smelled
of rusted locks, match strikes. Thus,
I never learned olfaction
properly—fond of the scent
of gas station as much as bakery.
In school: all the perfumes
of Arabia could not wash
Lady Macbeth's hands
of blood. At church: Joseph's
brothers sold him to merchants
bearing spice and myrrh.

But here in this Vermont inn,
a nude oil painting of a woman
in the bath, hangs above the towel
rack like a gender crucifixion.
I float restrained
in the small porcelain tub.
It is like a coffin of water.
The odalisque and I are no mere
bathroom selfies, a stay against
anxiety, trying to love
our bodies. The elusive male gaze
floats in from the ether
on steam, watches our ritual

grooming from the far away
bastion of antiquity's scrutiny—
*The Great School of Athens.*

The aqua wallpaper skins
from the wall's surface,
light reflecting off water,
my hot pink robe. Madness
leaks. The ruse and reverie
of my toilette has pruned me
into the woman I am now,
a bather immersed, breasts
rising like regimes from
an army of bathers, freed
from the prison of forever
sponging necks in a Degas.

The bathwater absorbs
my bone's dried violet
scent and architecture,
nanoparticles of wet ferns.
In the hydrogen, oxygen, I float on.
The water washing me
in places I only let God
perfume: his voyeuristic thrill
of this secrecy.

# Driving Home up Poker Hill I Consider: *So What*

My mind's a phone ringing
off the hook, a black phone cut
off from the root

of a Plath poem. Sometimes it rings so loudly
it sounds like silence because I'm used to it—
it sounds like:

*So what.*

The winding road, tree lined, was gorgeous in the rearview.
Don't wreck the car ogling *it* or saying so *what.*

Freud tried to define dreams and could only think
about sex.

What do I want,
a medal?

Resolving to be kinder to old folks, veterans, people in chains.
*So what.*

I am building a ship and it is difficult.

I am building it out of blood and notebooks.

I am building it so that it can sail through dissociations.

And if my kidney is salvaged for a sixteen year old. *So what.*
Jesus on the cross and they banged those nails

so hard. Crisis is
brought to birth by time.

Not knowing I was a character hasn't prevented me
from being one:

I am that girl running tattered through the pine forest.

I am that woman banging the hammer with a red handle.

I am building a safe room called a poem.

I am welding together steel walls, retrofitting, reinforcing.

I am trying to crack the secure code, collect provisions to last
a hundred years:

I can write because my index finger is *so*

and my pen is *what*

# Poem with Atoms in It

Dust motes on air          the sun arriving
in the window cracked          open, ferns, irises,

the idea of "freshness" and "complexity" &          June rising in Vermont,
Green Mountain, from the French. The windowpane          paint peels

the scent of tin and Russian leather and cold marble.
The irises beneath     smell of a forgotten          thought,
purpled with bruises
fresh with blood.          Each spray is a remembrance,
writing a spritzed nosegay of atoms.

Synesthesia makes me insane. Ferns have no scent. I think
therefore I smell.          The scented world
that has lost interest in perfume
portraits of a rose or violet or an orange blossom.

Now scent's          a glorious abstraction,
a Frankenthaler painting          hanging
On Fifth Avenue     or a bubbling Coca-Cola     in a New York School poem.
What is          an atom

but a work of art,     everywhere at once,
defying ekphrasis? This poem     disperses my existence,
separating it          into parts—words, sprays,
dots of color, scents. It's in this way form can
enact. What is content
but that which produces          atom by atom
a sum of the parts          rather than the whole?

SPRAY 2

An afternoon in the park made of Seurat's points
                pointing toward a new century,
the scent of walked-on grass.
                        A fine lady wearing a bustle and a hat,
a picnic, a summer day.
        When I think of atoms
I smell my grandfather, in charge of procuring the uranium
                for *The* Bomb. How he would,
tutoring me in chemistry,
        have a *Bulletin of Atomic Scientists* explanation
of the creation and destruction pointillism makes
        as we stand in the museum. How to split that atom
                        represented in a better way, maybe that's the point
of this education. He steers me toward art instead of atoms or men.
        Richard Feynman and his theoretical physics says
                        *they jiggle, always jiggling, jiggling.*
I want to change reality the way my sense of scent changes
        into colors, so that men can love me, as I interpret the nucleus
of scent, not as a cover-up but a desire.


SPRAY 3

The day is deodorized                Dr. Anne's room, in hospice,
                who opened    the Bible to *Song of Songs*
for this scientist who has no lover? Her brain's stem in the nose
                can't receive its syllables of scent,
can't name the world by its attendant atoms,
        that long poem, phrasing of molecules
she can't feel now      through the vibration
                theory of the scent of everything                here
        where the functional scent is        made up to erase the human body
in sickness and health        that marriage long over        we are killing
        germs, as outside the flowers are trying to spread

their DNA through scent. Moths fly by with rips
on wings we can't see, so infinitesimal, like mine
      as she once warned me not to fly toward that porch light

in his darkness, which was its own smell, its own
      perfume, filled with a complexity of notes.
        I went toward it like a hell-cat civet-laced pheromone,
Cuir de Russie or Peau d'Espagne, a colonialism of spices
      smelling of leather torture      gloves      men and horses
like some love stories      smell lacks morality.

He liked the idea of "Fresh"      the ways it applied to scent
      like Lucretius, he did not like the smell of women.
Like Lucretius he understood that everything we did was
      artifice and edifice: interstellar space, the kitchen, the bed,
the duration of time    my seventy cents to his dollar.
      For we are "aged, paltry things." Even Lucretius
when he wrote of the "malodorous mistress,"
                             pre-Summer's Eve douche,
how he preferred jacking off back when they fumigated
      the caverns from which life came.

Lucretius's *The Nature of Things,*
         Grandfather once told me standing in that museum smelling
of 4711 aftershave and the cigar-infused dread of how he made death,
        told us everything (before Christ) is made of quarks, neutrons, protons,
everything in orbit. Even love.
      *We come and go speaking. . . .*


SPRAY 4

In Seurat's *A Sunday Afternoon on the Island of La Grande Jatte*
everything smells better with leisure,            I float away
      with each umbrella.    Guerlain is on the scene
as that century opened its lemony verbena

                    and polished silver
of immortality, the same turn of the century
                    Niels Bohr had,        asking myself, flunking chemistry, what is a
configuration of atoms                 jiggling                existence,
                    but a kind of pointillist painting that started

the whole matter of matter's discussion off? Form
                    informs content, Levertov said and my teachers repeated.

My French other mother would remind me:
                    Gabrielle "Coco" Chanel—
just born somewhere nearby as water lilies Monet'd by—
          made Chanel N° 5, the abstract idea of modern womanhood in a bottle.
My form should be slim. I thought I should        be
          *I Dream of Jeannie.*               Your wish is my command, Sir.
                    O Astronaut! I never posed for an odalisque
with ripe peaches and cardamom pods. Let my ocean be
          alluring. (Portraiture

so out of fashion once, Seurat made the electron surround the nucleus
          with his paint brush on canvas,
                    not intuitive but ordered, precise as science.
Close brought it back.)

I spray an atomizer of Opium on the black dress
          for Anne's funeral. I remember all this, I am attendant parts

of a whole. With my atomizer I am dispersing the sadness of roses,
          like Mother Mary does when she comes
on visit, the smell of blooms everywhere,

          or how the dead return to us and we know by their sudden
perfume, how they are with us in the car or the art gallery not sure
nor, supposedly, love. I think I will await Anne's muguet scent.

In the old days, bathroom
          attendants offered a spritz of a facsimile. In the old days
I jumped on the trampoline, my synesthesia a parade of confetti . . . . .


SPRAY 5

My synesthesia a disorganized essay.
          My synesthesia
that pointillist painting on the T-shirt
          my atom bomb gramps bought me,
a mosaic        of starlight-tree sap-river water-bonfire.

My synesthesia the spray of atoms
                    from the Chanel Gardenia,
          or the Frederic Malle Portrait of a Lady
or                                        French Lover
          where I see green and hear Frank Sinatra and I'm in love
again with you and you and you and the sky.
                    Morning coffee softens
the edges. My synesthesia
          knows hot is hot,              the taste of cherries, myrrh,
mandarin, that the summer's orbit is
                              scent of balsam, grasshopper.

My synesthesia the clear blue sky in the Yukon the day
          my grandfather figured out
how to get the uranium to the desert. My synesthesia is the smell
          of his tobacco, the chlorine from his swim,
is his fishing hat on my head at the beach. My synesthesia all that
          DNA. My synesthesia the mixed-up atoms reordering

a Seurat painting as it comes alive
          atom-by-atom, point by point. The smell
of turpentine turning to Shalimar              on the air, wafting
                    by the café you sit at

whoever you are, dear reader, you are the art
                that ekphrasis can only describe by color harmony
or mélange optique smelling of wood moss and summer hay
        to me, synesthete, when I make love my feelings are colors,

Rothkoesque, yet the merging
        of continuity and discontinuity
                giving warmth, permeating     the dots are individual,
together they are form: people, scene, lake, trees
                atoms come and go
into our lives. Seurat comes
        and goes into my life: a picnic, a lover, a stroll.
Traits are structures. The painting atomizes
                objects, small dots reveal the way
in which we might consider
                love, the sun's dust mote
the most romantic of atoms.

I keep taking things apart and then putting them together
                to find a thesis for love, to ask myself—
                        Why this painting always hangs
in my childhood. Look honey, grandmamma said,
        how dots make up the whole, and later
                all that acid, all those dots. My chicken pox.
My genetic memory.
                I am a science project.
And when I write about love I am spraying this bouquet
                of atoms whispering and wafting something gourmand-floral,
a soliloquy reconfiguring the picture to keep it fresh,
                that ultimate and indivisible, when I atomize myself—
a shattered mosaic
                        down into units, floral, woodsy,
an all-overness, beyond abstract
                expressionism as wet dots drip their atoms
through space toward the jugular vein of my neck,
        throb of my translucent underwrist. I am

reflected at the shrine of my makeup mirror
                        as I sit.
The overall unity of the surface
               of my face reflects back to me, atomizing—
the smallest unit of medieval time, another life
               I lived once,
equal to fifteen ninety-fourths of a second. A dust mote, too,

in a sunbeam that smells of tobacco and mahogany
                  reminds me
it is daytime again, night finally over,
                          and we are leaving
to go to the museum again where I am
                      a non-zero member of a Boolean algebra
that is not a union of any other elements until I close the dictionary
        and become something else. Like a large pine in San Tropez,
a tree of life, its woody bark perfuming the morning
               with its hypothetical particles. Smell my only constant
sense. And you all are part of it flying
           to nowhere, for smell is a molecule
               that is light enough to float away,
semi-volatile, a molecular weight
                        that rarely exceeds 260AMU.
What we cannot smell kills us quickly . . . and the light can destroy
              perfume, it must be kept in darkness like an evil thing,
turning to vinegar in the sunshine. Our genetic code decides
              how our receptors will understand
what scents the world around us.
       Olfaction is a kind of a metonymy,
perfume on the pulse point reaches faster,
                    sped on by         the exotic human heart.

# III. BASE NOTES

Musk, Steamer Trunk, Ylang-Ylang, Vetiver, Snow

# Object and Experience

It is stationary: TV its only scenery.
You want this *me* that is having *that* exercise experience.

There is no on-ramp or exit. It simulates varying terrain
and conditions. We go nowhere on this non-road.

It beeps phony miles and pretends hills,
as a woman fakes an orgasm with real gasping. You gave me

this, so I won't fatten up for the holidays,
so I won't morph into your ex-wife instead of your trophy.

Its setting is level-five incline, level ten-speed.
This thing you gave me knows a lot about process:

how far, how much energy burned—all stored in its little box.
Sometimes I get to wondering if I am the object and it is

the experience, having a life more transcendent and ergonomic
than mine. Inertia mimics the actual. It was easy to assemble.

The box keeps track of everything, the basics of speed equals distance/time.
It monitors my performance, my goals. I use the bike everyday.

I don't know if I am riding toward you or away.

# I'm Not Going to Knit You a Sweater

I'm not going to use a measuring tape across the creamy-Bernini
expanse of your Bic shaven chest, smelling of Giorgio
Armani: I will not measure the sides of your arms, darling,
not even for posterity's sake. My knitting needles
gather dust mites and other ideas. I count
one-two-three-etc., all the rows for accuracy's sake and gauge.

We listen to Joni Mitchell, who sings to her lover she wants to knit
him a sweater. You scoff: you think gifts are controlling. I certainly don't
want to control you with cable-knit stitches sewing us into this stupid winter,
making you itch in the window seat. *Fine,* knit one, purl one is not for you.
I'm not casting on, or off, not making stocking stitches or buying
silk skeins. I'm not for worsted wool or fisherman's knit. No. Not black or blue

or beige or yellow, too. I am not going to knit you a sweater.
Merry Fucking Christmas. I actually *like* Christmas.
How can I convince you, I do not want
to knit you a sweater or knit for you in general,
especially I don't want to knit you together. You say I'm the one

with loose skeins and hidden polyesters.
So there. Knitting only parameters of space,
I dwell in counting and casting off, and lose track,
and make something out of knots that wasn't
there before. I count inaccurately because the world mystifies
me with its presence, its heft as thick as Icelandic sheep
and blue as that sky of ponies and vanishing points
off to the North Atlantic. I am not going to knit you a sweater,

or even one of those knitted, weird tree scarfs some people craft
for decorations to scroll around the trunk of a poor tree.
So stupid. Then! Wow: a doe leaps out.
I was sad about the argument you started last night
with your Kool-Aid word salad and a stitch inside me dropped

into a God-sized volcanic crater in my chest.
I was driving listening to Joni Mitchell's "All I Want" thinking,
how you say I look like her when I'm dazed.
Thinking I am not going to, not, and then brakes

screeched like Joni, high and quick. I hit the deer
and she flailed-flailed-rolled, not dead, but not alive
*enough*. My car was miraculously not dented, only the light
put out: sweet doe of the headlight.
I had no gun to shoot her between the eyes.

I thought I could back up and speed up and really run
her over, put her out of the trance of this December
evening where I'm not knitting my thoughts straight.
I didn't have the guts to run her over
again. Then people started stopping in the dark five p.m.

of mid-December. I thought of my knitting needles
in the trunk—unused—how I wasn't strong enough to puncture
them through doe-skull, to drill for the oil of essence,
musk of brain. No weapon formed against us shall prosper.
I am the deer in this poem, I lived, made it to the other side,
but some part of me—what? I don't know.
I have no mercy, or maybe too much.

The Sheriff and animal control lady arrived with rifles.
So happy, giddy with adrenals, to hear ammo for once in my life.

# Fumigation

The door's made of gingerbread the rats have eaten through.

You finger your record albums like frigid women.

You could be more silent than silence without much of a fight.

I float, a red birthday party balloon you let go into the ozone hole.

How I once felt my life against yours, two pieces of burnt toast.

The town had zoned me for you, now I'm a wetlands—

You can't run your cable under my land anymore,

But there's nothing wrong with you, just as there's nothing wrong with the sky.

I hum like a propane heater, rusted, but operational.

Nothing loves the world the way a mortal soul can,

Yet, the very word *domestication* sounds like a zoo for housewives.

Once fumigation was a gynecological procedure.

Once you smelled of mint, of truth.

Once I loved you madly like a girl pirate,

Now I use my sword to pick up moldy, low-loft towels from the floor.

# Stalking Me Onomatopoetically

> He closed my legs like a book.
>
> —ANGELA CARTER


I sought a restraining order against the sociopathic
poem that kept pounding on the door of my mind at four a.m.,
rousing me with a slap on the face with its metaphysics
of sick lust and panic. The order was dated March 1, 2016.
A Thursday. Rainy. The sociopoem smelled of Paco Rabanne—
A Cologne for Men—and was devilishly handsome, so elegant,
so English-lyrically, well-anthologized, and attractive, seemed to have a form
that suggested well-bred content, an understanding of stanzaic
architecture, and deep image. Yet, this poem I loved had once tried
to stab Dorothy Parker at a dinner party. He had claimed
to have French kissed Helen Vendler *and* Allen Ginsberg.
How could I rationalize or reconcile my love for the poem?
The poem tried to kill me, too, with the same red child's scissors
once, then another time it was tar and feather, because, the poem said,
"I love you so much." On therapeutic advice I sought the restraining order
against the poem because it couldn't contain itself, pushed me
down with a conceit stronger than my fragile couplets, how
it leaked anaphora like anti-freeze, bluish over the page
and into my life uninvited, thinking it knew me
better than I knew myself. The poem's arguments were convincing,
but it was all fanciful diversion. A lie. All through the day
and all through the night: *that poem.* The poem telling me I looked fat
in my Lord & Taylor dress. So, I bit the poem's ear,
again and again, until it bled a scary personification of ears. Stalking
me onomatopoetically down the sidewalk to where I kept my secret
sonnet turns inside. I just wanted to take a nap in Brooklyn,
sleep inside my source material, that pale of settlement,
the origin and end of everything in my family. So that the end
of my suffering might bring an insight, but the poem
turned my nap in Brooklyn into a series of disturbing
and surreal faces that made me awaken into the possibility that
I was the one who was so wrong, so ruined, damaged,
unable to sing. Yet, sometimes, honestly, I loved

what the poem said, when it convinced me of my tyranny.
I wanted to let go. I wanted its untouchable love. I waited for the poem.
The sociopoem's persona looked like Sir Mick Jagger, wore leather
pants, had biceps, smelled literary and up all night,
like bay rum and old books. The poem had a spell over me,
its incantatory propulsion got into my blood and bile
with its rhythms that made my heart race. It mailed me
threatening letters, collages containing articles about what happens
to women my age, how they die, again and again
alone and withering, like a nasty old tree
from a St. Vincent Millay sonnet taught
in girl's boarding schools. I wrestled the poem
until it swore to bless me, but it blessed me
in a language that made me feel uncomfortable.
It wasn't a vowelic yawp. It was a brutal stuttering *ich*
that made me feel sick, unclean, subway ridden,
which gave the poem a great joy.

# Letter from American Airspace

The end of romance was what the teenage girl
was telling you about on a bench in the Jardin
in San Miguel de Allende, giving you T.M.I.,
but you realized she might need a Father who is not in heaven.
She gasps: *Tinder is even sleazier in Mexico, how could it be*
*nostalgic?* You listened the way your poems do when you write
them down in the cafés of Kerouac's time here. You are Angelico
Americano with Instagram-troubled children of your own back home.
You are the only man I know who seriously loves his wife. Dios mío.
Right now this makes you the best volta in any sonnet. Yearning
is a kind of loss, a desire that's never filled. It is the drunk to his drink.
Never enough. Victim or victorious? Chasing yearning, I have discerned,
is like chasing a kind of poison. The *Popol Vuh* says in the beginning
there were corn people here, and love was a YES at every turn against
death. The end of romance knows this, no love letters, no mysteries,
holding out for another swipe, like a pull at the casino. The sun texts
its setting over the city. Back home children shoot other children.
Screens in every face. Savagery in the invisible, the Holy Ghost
weeping over new desires. My young female friend told me how nuclear
her hook ups are, how they like to choke and shag. Isn't it *not* romantic.
My hairdresser confirms the same story. I think I am lonelier
than lonely, for which there is no word or Proustian reference. I drown
and swoon in Mariachi music with no relief. May tenderness deliver
us. Maybe the only recall I have is this, my other friend home safely
from Afghanistan, telling me of the surgical tents where the world is
like triage and you order the grunts to lay it down, those who are
the chorus screaming: *unfuck it, unfuck this.*

# Judith Perfumes Herself

after Judy Chicago's Judith setting at *The Dinner Party*

*What exhilaration to tell a God-approved lie,*
Judith thought, bejeweled and holy scented,
as she beheaded Holofernes and saved her people.
An honored place at *The Dinner Party* has been set
for her now in the 20th century, a Last Supper
for the foremothers, a hand-painted porcelain
plate, a blooming floral vulva, layers of shadow
and light, her goblet full of the blood of Holofernes.
The elegance of ritual. In another room, her maid
from the 1610 Artemisia Gentileschi painting
waits to come to the dinner party carrying
a bowling ball bag with Holofernes's head in it,
expression still and looking like it had been
mansplaining the desires war makes on men,
and on Judith who had come bearing
her fragrant skin, newly perfumed, like a soul.
Her country besieged by the Assyrian army.
Judith's prayer was adequate to the day:
*Please Lord make my lies believable.*
You only get so many windows.
Sometimes truth is a parable embroidered
with the finest stitches of Bethulia
on a table runner saving your place in the story.
Sometimes the truth is a triangle,
a symbol of strength sewn into our fabric
with the gold thread of the dowry maker.
Judith said: this, this is my body
and this, this is your blood, as she raised
a goblet to Holofernes. To defeat
the enemy we must entertain
our wild archetypal essence. But what is it
exactly? Judith's fancy dress and gargush?
The way coins are sewn into the table runner?

The mystery scent of royal ferns? The altars
prepared with frankincense to appease the God
we want to make us good liars? To be a wealthy
widow means you can save your people. Judith
raised the mighty sword, thrust through his neck,
her maid straddling him like a bull in a rodeo fight.

# Shorewood Hills

I have tried to listen. The trees whisper *how alive.*
All the lake's boulders below with their greeny moss,
great answers that sang cells, rings, fungi into tree root,
vast networks they connect heaven to earth.
How did you find me? Once, thirty years ago,
a tall oak thrashed your window, looked in on us,
so young, on the carpeted floor, conceiving
another and ourselves out of the moon
dappled oak shadow. How to be quiet enough to ask
the canopy above us like a tunnel
over our stunned middle age.

The oaks and pines and prairie once loved me
into a kind of extinction, a stripping,
the way a bear pulls away bark. It scared me,
so I walled myself in. I keep crying.
I thought you meant nothing
to me then. That the world meant nothing.
My distress was the shrill, horrible sound
of buzz saw. How I wouldn't speak to you or let you
come with me to the clinic not far from right here.
I didn't want you to think you had to stay
just because a child sprouted in me. I wouldn't give you
that choice. And now look at you.
I reach for the broken world. I wouldn't face
the truth. These trees arch their bodies
over us with their long discussions about time.

The trees move toward the light,
which is also toward each other,
felled yet live again,
bloom great bowls and blossoms.
I reach over to touch your arm,
the long limb of you.
The oak calls like God through time:

I recall the girl I was and still am,
all thick with sap and leaf and hubris.
I arrived here, un-Daphned myself back to you.
I have walked their mazes, with my dog,
to find the map of this world of root,
a halo. Child or no child,
so says this love.

# Guerlain: Imperiale (Bedroom), 1853

Dear Reader, Fellow Perfume Testers and Collectors, Parfum Editors, Shunned
Lovers Who Can No Longer Stand the Scents:

The world is too much with me—I said.
The sun was hot in the window. I hate hot sun in the window. It is stressful.

The bed's white sheets out of a study by Gaston Bachelard in the *Poetics of Space*.

This perfume my lover wore was first made in 1853. Um, okay, I say:

It's girlie perfume. He was sexy in it. Lemony.

And this, if it is anything, is the fight of the will with inattention,

a dare. The bottle of Imperiale has 69 bees on it, all stinging.

This perfume, Eau de Cologne, Imperiale, by Guerlain, known
as one of the Guerlainades, whose top notes are so *bavard* talkative:

bergamot, neroli, verbena, lemon, orange, and once it settles into the skin

makes heart notes of lavender,
until the base arrives at the end of cedarwood, Tonka bean, reminding
that the future has come and is leaving soon.

Made by His Majesty's Royal Perfumer on the Rue de Rivoli in Paris:
It came out three years after Wordsworth died,

in honor of Napoleon III's wife Eugenie. But at that moment
the robust and citrusy scent meant I could cry.

I was a Romantic, and he had no idea what that meant.

He wrote messages about other women he planned to sleep with
on the public perfume blog. He had me in this musky trance.

I disassociated a bit on the wind of scents, and made
no sense anymore, for a while.

(If you are not Dearhearted, do not bother reading this, Dear Reader.)

Me, the once eight-year-old girl sticking a needle
in her index finger over and over,

how I taught myself not to cry. Years ago now
when after I was contained in my alone box, my house of no food, gone parents,

I'd walk downtown to the perfume shop where the Swedish saleswoman
let me luxuriate in the glow of glass and crystal, Windex and atomizers,

pretending to care. But no one cares really. Perfume is a cover up.

Perfume is about making sex not private. Perfume is about "smell me"
no matter if you want to or not. Seduction. Sedition. To some
with allergies, a belligerence.

Maybe it was in the confines of this scented space I first smelled the freedom
of Guerlain, and it reminds me now that I have escaped, and makes him seem
safe,

the way I smell him before I realize I smell him, his cage surrounding him.
He is part of the inner dialogue I have been corresponding with since then—
I'm not sure how he found me.

When the beautiful soul dies it smells of roses everywhere.
He kept me topsy-turvy, changing scents every four dates,
to continually disrupt and introduce new narrative.

He kept throwing me off his trail, with his scent.

Or maybe the number four, connected . . . to . . . was part of . . . his
mathematical mind, which I knew nothing about and when I said I could not
do math he'd go mad.

"Yes you, can." I can count syllables, spondees, who cares about trig or calc.

My French stepmother was once the Givenchy lady at Lord & Taylor,
and my sister in charge of spraying customers with new scents
as they walked into 1986 where Elvis Costello still jams and cabarets.

You see dearheart, dear reader, dear person who might be
kind: I had spent my wad of will. *Just give it to me, baby.*

I had been his Chanel girl. This gave me entrée. Later
he said he would marry the Guerlain shop girl at Bergdorf's.

Just joking. But, not. I would warn her later.

When I'd read the five-year restraining order, all the lurid details
of how he beat the Shalimar out of his five-foot wife from Nantes.

He marketed to me who he was and is and could be. His Guerlain bees:
I craved to be stung. Who are you to me,
he'd think, and pick a fragrance from his hundred bottles,

and manila envelopes of samples from Midwestern housewives
who were actually beautiful and sad. People
he met on his blogs. He had already charged me
with his leathery buttery bergamot, his old-school Dior Fahrenheit,

mixed with the layers of his original scent, a case in archeology. O discovery
is treacherous if sexy. The limbic risqué dance of my desire got away from me,

made me obsess on the scent of him, so soon he seemed to be everywhere,
in the coffee shop, on my sleeve, in the pineal glands, and in my nose hairs.

"The rarest blooms mix their soft perfumes," Baudelaire said in his poem
"Invitation to the Voyage," fifteen years after Imperiale appeared.

I have set sail, no going back
even if the earth ends because it is flat in the imagination of this love story.
The lightweight of this scent, how it is friendly in its top notes, gathers us
beside each other. I am full.

He knew the limbic system, how the ancient brain, full of procreative and fearful
urges, was attached to smell, processed the upshot
and how it would react before you or I were even aware.

He is that deviously smart. Like Antaeus or Egoïste, both by Chanel.

The way he used structural or behavioral patterns
to establish me inside his kingdom.

Wordsworth wouldn't have approved. He liked the natural
world, not the idea of the natural world. And Dear Reader,
I wanted him the way I wanted to kill myself as a child,

and later at other times, a deep merging into the hills
and lakes unknown, the ultimate petit mal. Mysterious O.
Dear Reader, Dearheart, How do I unlove him?

I am writing a spell to undo the alchemy
of his smells. Dear Reader, I'm foolish in my Cristalle, my No. 19,
my Estée Lauder mascara, my skinny jeans, my thwarted desires,
that light on the bed and his cheekbones. I ordered a novel on Amazon

about a guy who is a sociopath murderer of women,
a perfume-obsessed man. I read: *There was only one thing
the perfume could not do. It could not turn him into a person
who could love and be loved like everyone else.*

After the theater one night, he told me
over Sinatra, steaks, and iceberg salads,
his uncle killed his aunt. Then the next day told me he was surprised
my last boyfriend (who didn't like it if I ate ice cream)
hadn't killed me. How lucky I was!

This lemony summer scent is the one he wore that day.
We had made love for the first time, after the book award gala

where my book almost but didn't win, and in the morning
he was going on a date with someone else. I figured it out.

Still I went to breakfast with him. Maybe I wouldn't had I won
the award. The darkness, Dear Reader, is that everyone,
everyone is so beautiful once. The indent in the center of his chest,
where possibility resides. The thick horsehair of his head. Long finger
pushing the atomizer.

Dear Reader, too much psychotherapy,
no match for the Imperiale scent constructed
of the idea of summer light and the beauty of women in dresses
and men in seersucker with straw hats by a pond that one sees
from a bed with white sheets.

The scent made me carnal,
it made me a kite tangled in a tree,
it made me a watercolor brush stroke, rose near gold
in a summer scene depicting Maine. Light on his white sheets.

There was the smell of sunshine and the smell of his meanness.

I loved him into my own moon-cratered soul and I fell
in darkness toward imagined moonlight inside the stark

September sunshine. And my will does not bring him back, Dear Reader,
dearhearted one, not even an alchemy of scent can reconjure.

So memory comes, and so a memory goes, pollinating
other flowers for other lives.

Now that smell of lemons seems sour and sad.
Not the lightness effervescent. The sunlight changed

on the bed, my atoms stirred and mixed like martinis,
shaken. O Being! I look out the window, a chickadee
flies into my face. Crashes into glass. Falls, and falls.

And the bees are loose
again.

At that moment, I'd rather die under his hand than of lung cancer or slow pain.

O dearhearted Reader, do not try to help me:
*Now we're getting dressed again. Au Revoir.*

They will know him by this smell:

Imperiale!

# ACKNOWLEDGMENTS

Grateful acknowledgement is made to the editors of the journals who first published the following poems. The poems, sometimes in different versions, appeared as follows:

"Shulammite": *American Poetry Review*; "Lying Perfume Bottle of Chanel Pour Monsieur": *Bennington Review*; "Judith Perfumes Herself": *The Coachella Review*; "Letter from American Airspace": *The Common*; "In Vilnius": *Colorado Review*; "Shorewood Hills": *The Cortland Review*; "Burlington Is Nuts Today" and "Things that Aren't Good": *Electric Literature*; "In the Shadow": *Forklift, Ohio*; "A Warning": *Handsome*; "Stalking Me Onomatopoetically" and "The Girl from Ipanema": *Los Angeles Review*; "Hidden in Plain Sight" and "E-Diptych": *New Ohio Review*; "Fumigation": *New South*; "Killing Rabbits": *Pank*; "Object and Experience" and "The Box": *Pleiades*; "I'm Not Going to Knit You a Sweater" and "Driving Home up Poker Hill I Consider: *So What*": *Plume*; "Ars Poetica": *PORT (England)*; "Cinema Verité: Scenes 1, 2, 3, 5": *Post Road and Slope*; "Escape": *Salt Hill*; "Atomizer": *Seneca Review*; "Spritz": *SWWIM (Supporting Women Writers in Miami)*; "When the Insemination Man Comes to the Farm" and "An Alabaster Jar of Nard": *Tupelo Quarterly*; "Poem with Atoms in It": *West Branch*; "Cinema Verité: Scene 4": *Zocalo Public Square*.

"E-Diptych" appeared in *The Pushcart Prize*, 2013; "At Old Yankee Stadium" appeared in *Heart of the Order: Baseball Poems*, edited by Gabriel Fried (Persea Books, 2014); "Escape" appeared in *AROHO (A Room of One's Own Foundation)* online.

This book is dedicated to the memory, life and work of ~ Dr. Anne M. Johnston, MD, neonatologist to the stars ~

I would like to thank the Hermitage Artist's Retreat Foundation for a generous residency that helped make finishing this book possible, as well as a Vermont Council on the Arts grant.

Thank you to the entire team at LSU Press, especially James Long and Neal Novak. Deep appreciation and love to Marjorie Minot and the Very Reverend Diane Nancekivell for their spiritual wisdom, creative genius, care, and love. I would also like to thank the following people for their inspirations, insights, intellectual rigor, friendship, and close reading: Angela Palm, Michael Jager, Olena Kalytiak Davis, Jenny Molberg, Erin Adair-Hodges, Adrie Kusserow, Barbara Murphy, Karla Van Vliet, Matthew Lippman, Steve Langan, Graham Foust, Kerrin McCadden, Didi and Major Jackson, and the Vermont School of Poetry. Many thanks also to the father of my children and artist extraordinaire, W. David Powell. Deep gratitude to Laurie Simmons for use of the cover art from a series I love. And a shout out to my dear friends Kimberly Rupertus-Robinson and Nancy Dwyer, Dr. Red Flag, my siblings Bird and Pickles, and my extended family for their support. And with abiding love and gratitude to my children and their spouses. And for everything, love to my Edwin, Hans Manske.

# NOTES

"Self-Portrait: Smell Me" is an ekphrastic response to the artwork of Martynka Wawrzyniak's installation *Smell Me*, an olfactory self-portrait. In a *Wired* magazine interview she noted: "I wanted to create a self-portrait that was completely stripped of the visual prejudice that we usually associate with judging a person, or judging a woman specifically."

Also an ekphrastic response, "Lying Perfume Bottle of Chanel Pour Monsieur" was inspired by Laurie Simmons and her "Lying Objects" series, especially *Lying Perfume Bottle.*

"An Alabaster Jar of Nard" quotes Baudelaire, as well as descriptions of the Baudelaire perfume produced by the perfumer BYREDO. From BYREDO's website: "The scent is an homage to the toxic poetry of the French symbolist writer. Like in his most famous volume, *The Flowers of Evil,* idle and eroticism intermesh in a vaporous haze: 'A lazy isle to which nature has given singular trees, savory fruits, men with bodies vigorous and slender, and women in whose eyes shines a startling candor.'"

The italicized lines in "Shulammite" refer to sections from "The Song of Songs".

"The Ordinary Scent of Reality" is for Aaron Wisniewski, olfactory virtual reality evangelist and CEO of OVR Technology.

CPSIA information can be obtained
at www.ICGtesting.com
Printed in the USA
LVHW021512110121
676219LV00011B/2398